YOU AND YOUR FAMILY

A SURVIVAL GUIDE FOR ADOLESCENCE

By Gail C. Roberts, B.Ed., M.A.
and Lorraine Guttormson, M.A.

Edited by Pamela Espeland

Free
Spirit®
PUBLISHING

10 9 8 7 6 5 4 3

Printed in the United States of America

Cover and book design by MacLean & Tuminelly

Free Spirit Publishing Inc.
400 First Avenue North, Suite 616
Minneapolis, MN 55401
(612) 338-2068

CONTENTS

Introduction v

Activity #1: What Shape Is Your Family In?.....................1

Activity #2: Changing Shape, Shaping Change 11

Activity #3: What If...15

Activity #4: Who's In Charge? 23

Activity #5: Family Focus..25

Activity #6: Send a Message 39

Activity #7: Your Family Portrait 41

Activity #8: How Does Your Family Work? 43

Activity #9: Family Chores and Responsibilities 47

Activity #10: Thinking About Adoption 49

Activity #11: Heredity and Environment 53

Activity #12: Your Heredity 55

Activity #13: Your Environment.................................57

Activity #14: How Well Do You Know Your Parents? 59

Activity #15: Learning About Your Parents 1 67

Activity #16: Can You Think Like a Parent?..................75

Activity #17: Learning About Your Parents 2 81

Activity #18: Predictions...87

Activity #19: Learning About Your Parents 3 93

Activity #20: A National Family Quiz 99

Your Notes and Thoughts 101

INTRODUCTION

You And Your Family: A Survival Guide for Adolescence has been designed for you, with respect for your uniqueness and your potential. Working through it won't always be easy. The activities call upon you to be honest with yourself, to be open to new ideas, and to be willing to grow.

We hope the activities will lead you to some exciting discoveries about yourself and the world around you. We hope they will help you to understand and accept yourself, and to become more understanding and accepting of others. We hope they will give you a sense of having some degree of control over your life, and ultimately free you to be the best person you can be.

Gail C. Roberts, B.Ed., M.A.
Lorraine Guttormson, M.A.
August 1990

WHAT SHAPE IS YOUR FAMILY IN?

Kids your age seldom have control over their own living arrangements, happy or unhappy.

Maybe you live with your *biological parents,* or maybe you don't even know them. (Most kids of adoptive parents have never met their biological parents.) Maybe you live with only one parent.

Maybe you live with your *biological siblings* (brothers and/or sisters who have the same biological parents as you do), or maybe you don't. Maybe you don't have any biological siblings.

Perhaps your parents (or parent) look after other children, too. Perhaps you are cared for by older sibling(s), other relatives, or older friends.

If you are *fostered* or live in a *group home,* you may be in either a *temporary* or a *permanent* living situation.

There are many different ways to live.
There are many types of families.

ACTIVITY 1

If you live with both of your biological or adoptive parents, you live in a *nuclear family*.

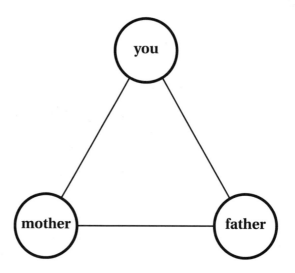

If you live with one of your biological parents, or an adoptive parent, you live in a *single-parent family*.

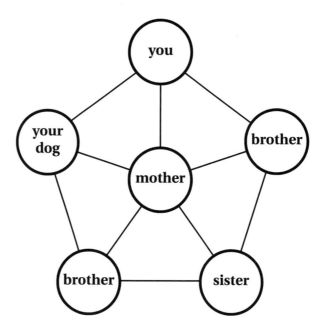

Maybe your parents are divorced, and you live with your mother. She has remarried, and your stepfather has children that are living with you, too. You live in a *blended family*.

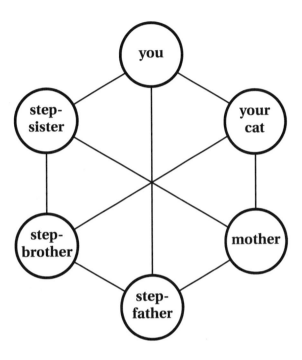

ACTIVITY 1

If your family includes three or more generations, you live in an *extended family*.

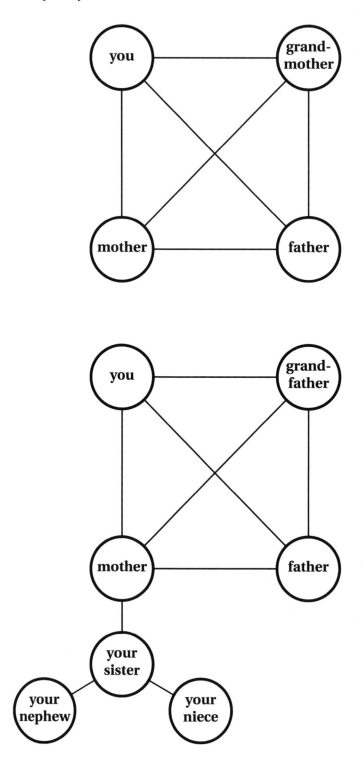

If you have biological, adopted, or fostered siblings, your living arrangement might look like this:

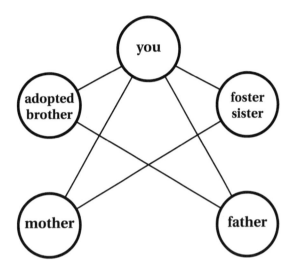

Maybe you live with your mother and her husband or boyfriend, and you see your dad for visits. He may have another wife or girlfriend with children who are now your stepbrothers and stepsisters.

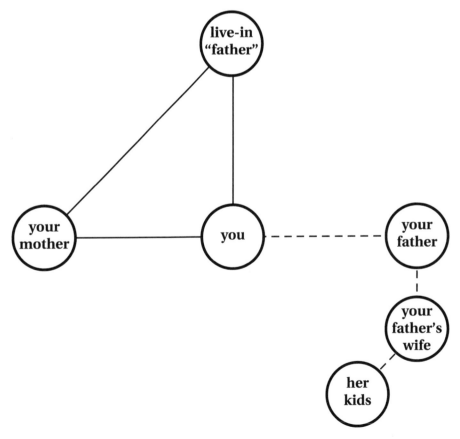

ACTIVITY 1

Maybe you live with your sibling(s) and your grandmother, and your parents visit you.

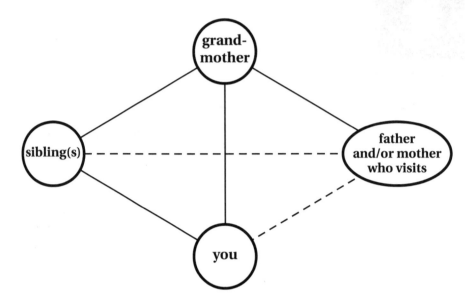

Maybe you live with your aunt and her cat, while your brother and sister live with your mother somewhere else.

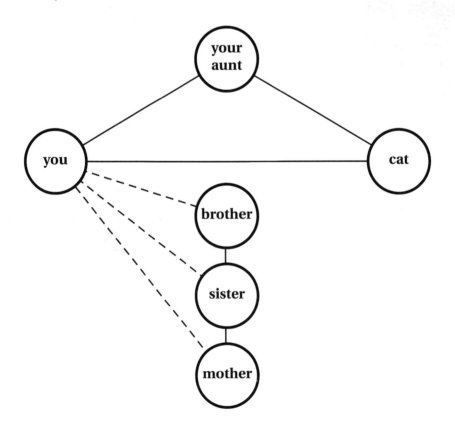

Maybe you are a foster child living in a foster family.

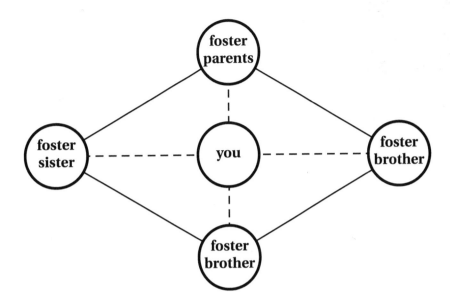

Maybe you live with your older sibling(s), apart from your parents.

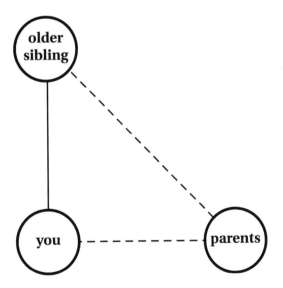

ACTIVITY 1

Maybe you and your sibling(s) live with your dad and his wife or live-in friend.

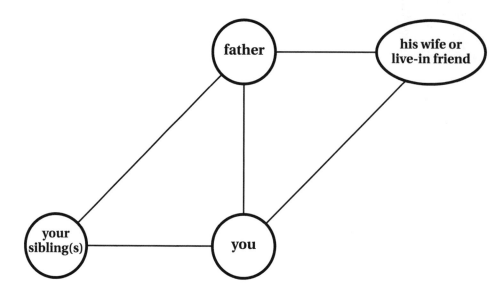

Maybe you live with both parents, but one of them has to travel for work and isn't around very often.

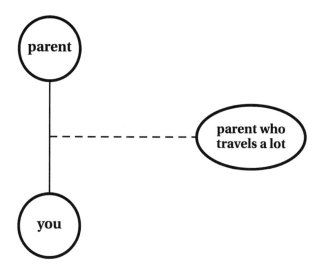

Maybe you live in a group home with adults and other children.

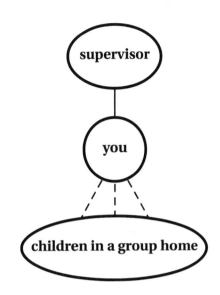

ACTIVITY 1

Draw your family's shape here.

CHANGING SHAPE, SHAPING CHANGE

There are many ways in which your family might change its shape. If your parents have a baby or adopt someone, you will have a new brother or sister. If your parent takes a new partner, you may suddenly have new stepbrothers or stepsisters. Or another relative or friend may come to live with you.

What other reasons can you think of that would cause a family's shape to change?

1. _____

2. _____

3. _____

4. _____

5. _____

6. _____

7. _____

8. _____

9. _____

10. _____

ACTIVITY 2

Did you think of these?

How many of these reasons did you think of that would cause a family's shape to change?

• The family may take in a foster child. (Parents contact a social agency in the community and make legal arrangements to give a child a temporary home.)

• A parent may accept short-term or long-term work in another city or country and return home whenever he or she can.

• The parents may divorce or separate.

• A family member may leave.

• A family member may return.

• The family may foster a child who lives in a foreign country. (The family sends money for food, clothing, medical care, education, and so on to a sponsoring organization. The family writes letters to the child to provide friendship and moral support.)

• A family member may be hospitalized for a long time.

• A family member may get or become a Big Brother or a Big Sister. (An adult and a child who are not related spend time together each week. There may be Big Brothers and Big Sisters organizations in your area.)

• The family may adopt a grandparent. (Community services sometimes match elderly persons with families. Or a family can make a point of visiting an older person in the neighborhood on a regular basis.)

• A family member may die.

• An immigrant family may stay with you until they get settled in their new country.

Things you should know about separation and divorce

Separation and divorce can be confusing and upsetting for kids. If they happen in your family, here are some things you should know.

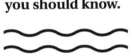

And here are some things you can do.

- You are not responsible for your parents' decision to separate or get a divorce.

- Your parents are certainly not separating or divorcing because of you. They may have many different reasons, but you are not one of them.

- Your parents are separating or divorcing because they are unhappy living together. They won't stop loving you and caring for you just because their living arrangements change.

- Ask questions so you understand what is going on. Tell your parents the things you are worried about or afraid of. If you have hurt or angry feelings, talk them out.

- If your parents won't talk about the separation or divorce, or if it seems to upset them when you do, try talking to a trusted friend, a relative, or another understanding adult.

- Try not to blame anyone. Things happen in life which aren't necessarily anyone's fault.

- Try not to choose sides. Although your parents no longer see themselves as husband and wife, they are still your parents, and they always will be. If you love them, be sure to let them know it.

- Don't let one parent use you as a tool or a weapon against the other. Avoid reporting to one parent what the other parent does or says.

- Know that if you and your parents can't decide what your new living arrangements will be, a court can — and it will decide with your best interests in mind.

- Try to realize that your parents are feeling emotionally stressed, too. They may be feeling insecure, rejected, guilty, anxious, or depressed. Even though you may be feeling unhappy, try to be as understanding as you can.

• At a time like this, it might be tempting to exploit your parents by making unreasonable demands or accepting "peace offerings." Don't do it, or someday you may regret taking advantage of the situation.

• Get (and give) as much support as you can from old family friends, and from extended family members like grandparents. Like you, they may be feeling helpless, hurt, and worried. On the other hand, if they put unfair pressure on you, avoid them. (For example, they shouldn't blame people, choose sides, or ask you to blame or choose sides.)

• Once the separation or divorce happens, get on with your life. After a while, you may find that your parents are happier and easier to get along with as individuals. You may find that you're happier, too. You may spend more time with one of your parents than you did before. You may feel more mature, and your parents may treat you like a more mature person. You may have more independence and responsibility than before.

• Plan to have a good family of your own someday. Learn how by spending time with friends who live in happy families. (Remember that families come in all shapes and sizes. There are happy nuclear families, happy extended families, happy blended families, and families that have gone through separation or divorce and are happy again in their new shapes.) Talk about families with your friends. Invite them over to your house.

Finally...

• There are some parents who simply don't want the responsibility of taking care of their families. There are some parents who feel that someone else will come along who can do a better job of being a parent. There are some parents who don't like family life. These parents may just leave, and they may not want to keep having a relationship with their children. If this happens to you, get on with your own life. There are many other people in this world who will love you and care for you. Look for them.

WHAT IF...

What if a member of your family decided to leave, or had to leave for some reason?

For this activity, think about each family member in turn. Imagine what life would be like if he or she left your family.

What special things does each person contribute to your family? What would your family miss if he or she left? What would your family gain? How would your family relationships change?

Answer the questions on the following pages as honestly as you can.

ACTIVITY 3

Family member's name: _____

1. What special things does this person contribute to your family?

   _____

   _____

   _____

2. What would your family miss if this person left?

   _____

   _____

   _____

3. What would your family gain if this person left?

   _____

   _____

   _____

4. How would your family relationships change if this person left?

   _____

   _____

   _____

Family member's name: _____

1. What special things does this person contribute to your family?

   _____

   _____

   _____

2. What would your family miss if this person left?

   _____

   _____

   _____

3. What would your family gain if this person left?

   _____

   _____

   _____

4. How would your family relationships change if this person left?

   _____

   _____

   _____

ACTIVITY 3

Family member's name: _____

1. What special things does this person contribute to your family?

   _____

   _____

   _____

2. What would your family miss if this person left?

   _____

   _____

   _____

3. What would your family gain if this person left?

   _____

   _____

   _____

4. How would your family relationships change if this person left?

   _____

   _____

   _____

Family member's name: _____

1. What special things does this person contribute to your family?

_____

_____

_____

2. What would your family miss if this person left?

_____

_____

_____

3. What would your family gain if this person left?

_____

_____

_____

4. How would your family relationships change if this person left?

_____

_____

_____

ACTIVITY 3

Family member's name: _____

1. What special things does this person contribute to your family?

   _____

   _____

   _____

2. What would your family miss if this person left?

   _____

   _____

   _____

3. What would your family gain if this person left?

   _____

   _____

   _____

4. How would your family relationships change if this person left?

   _____

   _____

   _____

Family member's name: _____

1. What special things does this person contribute to your family?

_____

_____

_____

2. What would your family miss if this person left?

_____

_____

_____

3. What would your family gain if this person left?

_____

_____

_____

4. How would your family relationships change if this person left?

_____

_____

_____

WHO'S IN CHARGE?

Whatever kind of family you live in, it helps to know exactly what's expected of you. And it helps to know what you have the right to expect in return.

For example, you should know who's responsible for seeing that you go to school. You should know if you're entitled to receive spending money (an allowance), how much, and how often. You should know what you are and aren't allowed to spend it on. You should know exactly what consequences to expect if you break any of the family rules.

In a *democratic family*, each member of the family has some say in establishing and enforcing family rules and making family decisions. In a *patriarchal family*, the father has this authority. In a *matriarchal family*, the mother has this authority.

Who's in charge in *your* family? Think about this as you answer the questions on the following page.

ACTIVITY 4

1. What kind of family do you live in — democratic, patriarchal, or matriarchal?

_____

If your family isn't any of these, then how are family rules and decisions made?

_____

_____

_____

_____

2. Is this satisfactory for everyone in your family? (Find out by asking them.)

_____

_____

_____

_____

3. If you wanted to change the way rules and decisions are made in your family, could you? If you could, what changes would you make?

_____

_____

_____

_____

_____

_____

FAMILY FOCUS

See your whole family in your mind. Imagine each person, one at a time.

Think about your memories of that person. Think about your feelings, likes, and dislikes. Be honest about your memories and your feelings.

Answer the questions on the following pages as honestly as you can.

ACTIVITY 5

Family member's name: _____

1. How long have you known this person?

_____

2. It's possible to love a person, yet hate the way he or she treats you. It's possible to love someone but not like him or her.

What do you feel about this person? Circle your answers on this continuum:

love   like   no feeling   dislike   hate

3. What do you like most about this person?

_____

_____

4. What do you like least about this person?

_____

_____

5. What's the best thing this person has ever done for you or to you?

_____

_____

6. What's the worst thing this person has ever done for you or to you?

_____

_____

7. What kinds of things do you tell others about this person?

_____

_____

_____

_____

8. What kinds of things do you think this person tells others about you?

_____

_____

_____

_____

9. What will you always remember about this person?

_____

_____

_____

_____

10. What will this person always remember about you?

_____

_____

_____

_____

ACTIVITY 5

Family member's name: _____

1. How long have you known this person?

   _____

2. What do you feel about this person? Circle your answers on this continuum:

   love   like   no feeling   dislike   hate
   |_____|_____|_____|_____|

3. What do you like most about this person?

   _____

   _____

4. What do you like least about this person?

   _____

   _____

5. What's the best thing this person has ever done for you or to you?

   _____

   _____

6. What's the worst thing this person has ever done for you or to you?

   _____

   _____

7. What kinds of things do you tell others about this person?

   _____

   _____

   _____

   _____

8. What kinds of things do you think this person tells others about you?

_____

_____

_____

_____

9. What will you always remember about this person?

_____

_____

_____

_____

10. What will this person always remember about you?

_____

_____

_____

_____

ACTIVITY 5

Family member's name: _____

1. How long have you known this person?

_____

2. What do you feel about this person? Circle your answers on this continuum:

love   like   no feeling   dislike   hate

3. What do you like most about this person?

_____

_____

4. What do you like least about this person?

_____

_____

5. What's the best thing this person has ever done for you or to you?

_____

_____

6. What's the worst thing this person has ever done for you or to you?

_____

_____

7. What kinds of things do you tell others about this person?

_____

_____

_____

_____

8. What kinds of things do you think this person tells others about you?

_____

_____

_____

_____

9. What will you always remember about this person?

_____

_____

_____

_____

10. What will this person always remember about you?

_____

_____

_____

_____

ACTIVITY 5

Family member's name: _____

1. How long have you known this person?

_____

2. What do you feel about this person? Circle your answers on this continuum:

       love   like   no feeling   dislike   hate

3. What do you like most about this person?

_____

_____

4. What do you like least about this person?

_____

_____

5. What's the best thing this person has ever done for you or to you?

_____

_____

6. What's the worst thing this person has ever done for you or to you?

_____

_____

7. What kinds of things do you tell others about this person?

_____

_____

_____

_____

8. What kinds of things do you think this person tells others about you?

_____

_____

_____

_____

9. What will you always remember about this person?

_____

_____

_____

_____

10. What will this person always remember about you?

_____

_____

_____

_____

ACTIVITY 5

Family member's name: _____

1. How long have you known this person?

    _____

2. What do you feel about this person? Circle your answers on this continuum:

    love   like   no feeling   dislike   hate
    |_____|_____|_____|_____|

3. What do you like most about this person?

    _____

    _____

4. What do you like least about this person?

    _____

    _____

5. What's the best thing this person has ever done for you or to you?

    _____

    _____

6. What's the worst thing this person has ever done for you or to you?

    _____

    _____

7. What kinds of things do you tell others about this person?

    _____

    _____

    _____

    _____

8. What kinds of things do you think this person tells others about you?

_____

_____

_____

_____

9. What will you always remember about this person?

_____

_____

_____

_____

10. What will this person always remember about you?

_____

_____

_____

_____

ACTIVITY 5

Family member's name: _____

1. How long have you known this person?

_____

2. What do you feel about this person? Circle your answers on this continuum:

      love   like   no feeling   dislike   hate

3. What do you like most about this person?

_____

_____

4. What do you like least about this person?

_____

_____

5. What's the best thing this person has ever done for you or to you?

_____

_____

6. What's the worst thing this person has ever done for you or to you?

_____

_____

7. What kinds of things do you tell others about this person?

_____

_____

_____

_____

8. What kinds of things do you think this person tells others about you?

_____

_____

_____

_____

9. What will you always remember about this person?

_____

_____

_____

_____

10. What will this person always remember about you?

_____

_____

_____

_____

Something to think about

When you were doing Activity #5, Family Focus, did you think of anything you'd like to tell one or more of your family members?
    Do you think you will tell? Why or why not?
    If you think you won't tell, is there anything that could change your mind?

SEND A MESSAGE

Sometimes there are things we want to say, but it's hard to say them out loud. It's easier to write them down.

If you have things to tell your family members, think about making cards for them. (You can even make cards for yourself.)

Here are some examples of things you could say. Or make up your own messages. Be sure to write "To: _____" and "From: _____" on each card.

- World's Best Friend

- World's Worst _____

- World's Best _____

- I Love You Because _____

- Why did you _____? It upset me a lot!

- World's Best Parent

- World's Best Pet

- How about a hug?

- Thank you for _____

- It makes me happy when you _____

- It makes me sad when you _____

- I am sorry that I _____. Please forgive me.

- I hate it when you _____

ACTIVITY 6

*World's
Best
Friend*

To: _____

From: _____

*World's
Worst*

_____

To: _____

From: _____

*World's
Best*

_____

To: _____

From: _____

To: _____

I Love You Because

_____

From: _____

*How about
a hug?*

To: _____

From: _____

To: _____

Why did you _____
_____ **?**

It upset me a lot!

From: _____

YOUR FAMILY PORTRAIT

Draw your family portrait in the picture frame. Or use the next page to draw an even bigger family portrait. Sign and date your portrait.

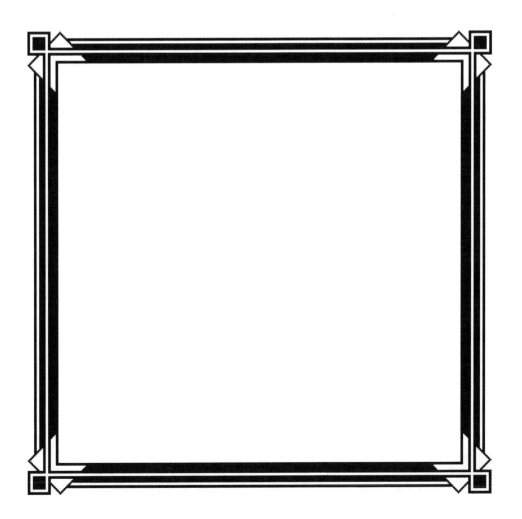

ACTIVITY 7

HOW DOES YOUR FAMILY WORK?

Before trying this activity, you may want to review Activity #4: Who's In Charge? on pages 23–24.

1. How does your family decide to make a major purchase? (Examples: a house, a car, major repairs.)

_____

_____

2. How does your family decide what standards of behavior are acceptable for family members? How are consequences and discipline determined?

_____

_____

3. How does your family make holiday or travel plans? How often does your family take vacations?

_____

_____

4. How often does your whole family eat meals together? Are there any times when the whole family gets together for a special meal or occasion?

_____

_____

5. Does your family have any "family traditions" or rituals? (Examples: an annual camping trip, measuring a child's height on his or her birthday, anniversaries.)

_____

_____

6. Does your family have any strong beliefs? (Examples: cultural beliefs, religious beliefs, social commitments, environmental concerns.)

_____

_____

7. Does your family have any special problems to work out? (Examples: a terminally ill member, an addicted or abusive member.) Who takes responsibility for solving problems like these?

_____

_____

8. What's the "division of labor" around your house? Who is responsible for what chores or duties, and who decides?

_____

_____

Something to think about

Who in your family cleans the toilet bowl? Changes the baby's diapers? Recycles the garbage? Changes the cat's litter box, or cleans up after the dog? Why do these family members do these particular chores? Who would do them if they didn't?

9. Do you see any members of your extended family often or regularly? Who? What does this mean to you? (Examples: grandparents, a favorite aunt or uncle.)

_____

_____

_____

10. What activities do you do with members of your family? Which family members? How often? Add your own examples to this list.

a. watch TV _____

b. go shopping _____

c. play sports _____

d. fight _____

e. sing, play music, listen to music _____

f. play games _____

g. build or fix things _____

h. drive around _____

i. go to the movies _____

j. take walks _____

k. argue _____

l. just hang out together _____

m. read _____

n. worship _____

o. _____

p. _____

q. _____

r. _____

ACTIVITY 8

11. How do family members' jobs affect your family? (Examples: Working different shifts, hours of employment, seasonal jobs, quitting or getting fired or laid off, looking for work, starting a new job.)

_____

_____

_____

12. Think about where your family lives. (Examples: city, country, or suburb; by an ocean or lake, on an island, in the mountains or on the prairie; a northern or southern climate.) How does this affect your family?

_____

_____

_____

13. When you're an adult with your own family, what things will you want to be the same as they are in your present family? Why?

_____

_____

_____

14. What things will you want to be different about your future family? Why?

_____

_____

_____

15. Are there things about your family you'd like to change right now? Do you think it's possible to change them? Why or why not?

_____

_____

_____

FAMILY CHORES AND RESPONSIBILITIES

The division of labor — who's responsible for what chores and duties — is often a point of conflict in families.

How are jobs and chores assigned in your family? Who decides which family members will do what? Do family members sit down together and talk about it, or does one person make all the decisions for everyone?

Complete the chart on the following page. Does your family's arrangement seem fair to you? Why or why not?

ACTIVITY 9

How often are you responsible for each of these?

	Always	Often	Sometimes	Never
1. Fixing a meal	☐	☐	☐	☐
2. Washing your clothes	☐	☐	☐	☐
3. Getting yourself out of bed in the morning and ready for the day	☐	☐	☐	☐
4. Setting or clearing the table	☐	☐	☐	☐
5. Doing the dishes	☐	☐	☐	☐
6. Being where you're supposed to be — on time!	☐	☐	☐	☐
7. Cleaning your room	☐	☐	☐	☐
8. Cleaning the house	☐	☐	☐	☐
9. Shopping for your clothes	☐	☐	☐	☐
10. Shopping for groceries	☐	☐	☐	☐
11. Caring for the family pet	☐	☐	☐	☐
12. Taking out the garbage, recycling	☐	☐	☐	☐
13. Babysitting your siblings	☐	☐	☐	☐
14. Doing errands	☐	☐	☐	☐
15. Working outside (Examples: shoveling snow, cutting grass, working in the garden)	☐	☐	☐	☐

What other kinds of work do you contribute to your family?

_____

What other kinds of work could you or should you contribute to your family?

_____

THINKING ABOUT ADOPTION

Were you adopted, or do you know someone who was adopted?

If you were adopted, your parents have probably told you. But some kids who haven't been adopted think they *must* have been because they couldn't *possibly* be a part of the family they're in! This irrational belief is so common that it has an official name: the Changeling Syndrome. If you have any doubts about where you came from, ASK.

If you really were adopted and you don't know your biological parents, it's natural for you to wonder about them. Your adoptive parents may be willing to help you find out what you want to know. Pick a quiet, private time and place to talk about this with them. Explain that you're ready to investigate the circumstances of your adoption.

It's possible that your adoptive parents may feel hurt by your interest in your biological parents. They may feel that you want to find your biological parents because they aren't "good enough," or because they have "let you down" in some way. Be sensitive to their feelings of jealousy or rejection.

If your adoptive parents are reluctant to help you, or if they don't know anything about your biological parents, what next? If you're still curious, there are places you can go for information. This information may not be released to you until you are of legal age. When you're old enough, there are organizations you can register with. If your biological parents register, too, the organizations may help you get in touch with each other.

How do you feel about adoption — and about children? Find out by answering the questions on the following pages.

ACTIVITY 10

1. What do you think of adoption? How do you feel about it?

_____

_____

_____

2. Would you want your family to adopt a pet? a baby? a toddler? an older child? a grandparent? Why or why not?

_____

_____

_____

Something to think about

Many children need homes. Adoption agencies and adoption lawyers have long waiting lists of people who are willing to adopt infants, but it's much harder to place children over two years of age, siblings who want to stay together, children who have disabilities, and children of certain races.

3. Do you plan to have biological children when you are an adult? Why or why not?

_____

_____

_____

4. Do you plan to adopt children when you are an adult? Why or why not?

_____

_____

_____

5. Do you plan to be a foster parent when you are an adult? Why or why not?

_____

_____

_____

6. Do you plan to help support a needy child who lives in your country or another country when you are an adult? Why or why not?

_____

_____

_____

7. Which of these ideas would you like to talk to your present family or friends about?

_____

_____

_____

Pick an appropriate time and place to talk about these ideas.

HEREDITY AND ENVIRONMENT

A

Imagine that identical twins are separated at birth. They grow up in two different families in the same town. Twelve years later, they are reunited.

In what ways do you think they will be alike?

_____

_____

_____

_____

_____

_____

In what ways do you think they will be different?

_____

_____

_____

_____

_____

_____

_____

ACTIVITY 11

Imagine that the twins grow up in two different countries with very different cultures.

In what ways do you think they will be alike?

_____

_____

_____

_____

_____

In what ways do you think they will be different?

_____

_____

_____

_____

_____

YOUR HEREDITY

Each of us has a *genetic heritage.* We have inherited certain genes from our parents, grandparents, and great-grandparents (and even farther back). These genes give us specific physical characteristics and, sometimes, specific abilities.

Think about your biological relatives. Which ones do you think "passed down" certain genes to you? Other people in your family may be able to help you gather this information about your genetic heritage.

If you are adopted or fostered, ask your adoptive parents to tell you what they know about your biological parents. If they can't or won't do this, think about all the people in your adoptive or foster family. Which ones are you most like? Which ones do you most resemble?

Fill in the chart on the next page with information about your genetic heritage. There's also a column ("Me") for characteristics that don't seem to "come from" anybody — they seem to be yours alone.

Note: Your *maternal grandparents* are your mother's parents. Your *paternal grandparents* are your father's parents.

ACTIVITY 12

My Genetic Heritage

	Me	My mother	My father	My maternal grandmother	My maternal grandfather	My paternal grandmother	My paternal grandfather
eye color							
hair color							
height (tall, short, average)							
weight (heavy, thin, average)							
body type, build (small, medium, large)							
shape of nose (draw it!)							
size of feet (large, small)							
athletic ability							
scholastic ability							
artistic ability							
health							
other: _____							
other: _____							

Your ENVIRONMENT

Think about your *personality traits*. Where do you think they came from?

The people around us have a strong influence on how we think and behave. Parents, siblings, other relatives, friends, teachers, and neighbors help to shape our attitudes and actions. We're also influenced by people we don't know personally but often see: TV personalities; movie, music, and sports stars; actors in advertisements.

Fill in the chart on the next page with information about your environment. Write in the names of people in your life who have had (and still have) a strong influence on you. There's also a column ("Me") for personality traits that don't seem to "come from" anybody — they seem to be yours alone.

Note: You may want to ask someone who knows you well to help you do this activity.

ACTIVITY 13

My Environmental Influences

	Me	Name: _____	Name: _____	Name: _____	Name: _____	Name: _____	Name: _____
sense of humor							
temper (quick/slow to anger, quick/slow to forgive)							
sense of responsibility							
interests, hobbies, habits							
prejudices							
neatness							
generosity							
self-confidence							
kindness							
self-image							
other: _____							
other: _____							

How well do you know your parents?

When you live with people for a long time, you think you know them pretty well. Like your parents, for example. You may think you know just about everything there is to know about them — their likes and dislikes, how they feel about certain things, the important experiences in their lives, their hopes and dreams.

But how well do you *really* know your parents? The questions on the following pages can help you to find out. Answer as many as you can — *without* talking to your parents first.

ACTIVITY 14

YOUR MOTHER

1. Where was she born? _____

2. How old is she? _____

3. How does she feel about growing older?

_____

4. What is her favorite color? _____

5. What is her favorite food? _____

6. Who is her best female friend? Why?

_____

_____

Who is her best male friend? Why?

_____

_____

7. How does she feel about…

…her home town?

_____

…her own childhood?

_____

…her friends?

_____

…her possessions?

_____

…her work?

_____

…her children?

_____

8. What's the most wonderful thing she has ever done or experienced?

_____

_____

9. What's the most horrible thing she has ever done or experienced?

_____

_____

10. When your mother was young, what did she want to grow up to do or become?

_____

_____

Did she succeed? Why or why not?

_____

_____

How does she feel about this now?

_____

_____

11. What is your mother's greatest hope?

_____

_____

12. If she had a whole day to herself, what would she do?

_____

_____

ACTIVITY 14

13. If she had more money, what would she do?

_____

_____

What would she do if she had less money?

_____

_____

14. Imagine that you weren't around anymore. What would your mother do without you?

_____

_____

Imagine that your mother wasn't around anymore. What would you do without her?

_____

_____

YOUR FATHER

1. Where was he born? _____

2. How old is he? _____

3. How does he feel about growing older?

_____

4. What is his favorite color? _____

5. What is his favorite food? _____

6. Who is his best male friend? Why?

_____

_____

Who is his best female friend? Why?

_____

_____

7. How does he feel about…

…his home town?

_____

…his own childhood?

_____

…his friends?

_____

…his possessions?

_____

…his work?

_____

…his children?

_____

8. What's the most wonderful thing he has ever done or experienced?

_____

_____

9. What's the most horrible thing he has ever done or experienced?

_____

_____

10. When your father was young, what did he want to grow up to do or become?

_____

_____

Did he succeed? Why or why not?

_____

_____

How does he feel about this now?

_____

_____

11. What is your father's greatest hope?

_____

_____

12. If he had a whole day to himself, what would he do?

_____

_____

13. If he had more money, what would he do?

_____

_____

What would he do if he had less money?

_____

_____

14. Imagine that you weren't around anymore. What would your father do without you?

_____

_____

Imagine that your father wasn't around anymore. What would you do without him?

_____

_____

Something to think about

Do you know who would take care of you if your parents were to die? Have any specific arrangements been made? If so, what are they? Pick a quiet, private time and place to talk about this with your parents, if you think you should.

LEARNING ABOUT YOUR PARENTS 1

Before doing this activity, be sure to finish Activity #14: How Well Do You Know Your Parents? on pages 59–65.

Now interview your parents, asking them the questions on the following pages. (These are the same questions you asked yourself, only here they have been turned into interview questions.) Write down their answers.

Ask your parents if they'd like to interview you, too.

If you want to, you can also interview another family member or a friend.

ACTIVITY 15

YOUR MOTHER

1. Where were you born? _____

2. How old are you? _____

3. How do you feel about growing older?

_____

4. What is your favorite color? _____

5. What is your favorite food? _____

6. Who is your best female friend? Why?

_____

_____

Who is your best male friend? Why?

_____

_____

7. How do you feel about...

...your home town?

_____

...your own childhood?

_____

...your friends?

_____

...your possessions?

_____

...your work?

_____

...your children?

_____

8. What's the most wonderful thing you have ever done or experienced?

_____

_____

9. What's the most horrible thing you have ever done or experienced?

_____

_____

10. When you were young, what did you want to grow up to do or become?

_____

_____

Did you succeed? Why or why not?

_____

_____

How do you feel about this now?

_____

_____

11. What is your greatest hope?

_____

_____

12. If you had a whole day to herself, what would you do?

_____

_____

ACTIVITY 15

13. If you had more money, what would you do?

_____

_____

What would you do if you had less money?

_____

_____

14. Imagine that I wasn't around anymore. What would you do without me?

_____

_____

15. Imagine that you weren't around anymore. What would I do without you?

_____

_____

YOUR FATHER

1. Where were you born? _____

2. How old are you? _____

3. How do you feel about growing older?

_____

4. What is your favorite color? _____

5. What is your favorite food? _____

6. Who is your best male friend? Why?

_____

_____

Who is your best female friend? Why?

_____

_____

7. How do you feel about…

…your home town?

_____

…your own childhood?

_____

…your friends?

_____

…your possessions?

_____

…your work?

_____

…your children?

_____

ACTIVITY 15

8. What's the most wonderful thing you have ever done or experienced?

_____

_____

9. What's the most horrible thing you have ever done or experienced?

_____

_____

10. When you were young, what did you want to grow up to do or become?

_____

_____

Did you succeed? Why or why not?

_____

_____

How do you feel about this now?

_____

_____

11. What is your greatest hope?

_____

_____

12. If you had a whole day to yourself, what would you do?

_____

_____

13. If you had more money, what would you do?

_____

_____

What would you do if you had less money?

_____

_____

14. Imagine that I wasn't around anymore. What would you do without me?

_____

_____

15. Imagine that you weren't around anymore. What would I do without you?

_____

_____

CAN YOU THINK LIKE A PARENT?

How do your parents feel about being parents? How do they feel about being *your* parents? Have you ever asked them? For this activity, try thinking the way your parents do. Try seeing things from *their* point of view. Answer the questions on the following pages — *without* talking to them first. Whenever you see *(your name)*, that means YOU.

ACTIVITY 16

YOUR MOTHER

1. What's the best thing about being a parent?

_____

_____

2. What's the worst thing about being a parent?

_____

_____

3. What specific things do you like most about *(your name)*?

_____

_____

4. What specific things do you like least about *(your name)*?

_____

_____

5. What about *(your name)* makes you worry the most?

_____

_____

6. What plans or dreams do you have for *(your name)*?

_____

_____

7. What makes you glad that *(your name)* is growing up?

_____

_____

8. What makes you sad that *(your name)* is growing up?

_____

_____

9. Why do you seem to say "NO" so often?

_____

_____

10. Why do you seem to want to know everything about
(your name)'s life?

_____

_____

OR: Why don't you seem to care?

_____

_____

11. What did you do when you were young that you hope *(your name)*
WON'T do?

_____

_____

12. What did you do when you were young that you hope *(your name)*
WILL do?

_____

_____

ACTIVITY 16

YOUR FATHER

1. What's the best thing about being a parent?

_____

_____

2. What's the worst thing about being a parent?

_____

_____

3. What specific things do you like most about *(your name)*?

_____

_____

4. What specific things do you like least about *(your name)*?

_____

_____

5. What about *(your name)* makes you worry the most?

_____

_____

6. What plans or dreams do you have for *(your name)*?

_____

_____

7. What makes you glad that *(your name)* is growing up?

_____

_____

8. What makes you sad that *(your name)* is growing up?

_____

_____

9. Why do you seem to say "NO" so often?

_____

_____

10. Why do you seem to want to know everything about
(your name)'s life?

_____

_____

OR: Why don't you seem to care?

_____

_____

11. What did you do when you were young that you hope *(your name)*
WON'T do?

_____

_____

12. What did you do when you were young that you hope *(your name)*
WILL do?

_____

_____

LEARNING ABOUT YOUR PARENTS 2

Before doing this activity, be sure to finish Activity #16: Can You Think Like a Parent? on pages 75–79.

Now interview your parents, asking them the questions on the following pages. (These are the same questions you asked yourself, only here they have been turned into interview questions.) Write down their answers. You may want to invite another family member or a friend to join you for the interviews.

After your interviews, compare your parents' answers with your answers. How accurate were your answers? How well can you think like a parent?

ACTIVITY 17

YOUR MOTHER

1. What's the best thing about being a parent?

   _____

   _____

2. What's the worst thing about being a parent?

   _____

   _____

3. What specific things do you like most about me?

   _____

   _____

4. What specific things do you like least about me?

   _____

   _____

5. What about me makes you worry the most?

   _____

   _____

6. What plans or dreams do you have for me?

   _____

   _____

7. What makes you glad that I'm growing up?

   _____

   _____

8. What makes you sad that I'm growing up?

   _____

   _____

9. Why do you seem to say "NO" so often?

_____

_____

10. Why do you seem to want to know everything about my life?

_____

_____

OR: Why don't you seem to care?

_____

_____

11. What did you do when you were young that you hope I WON'T do?

_____

_____

12. What did you do when you were young that you hope I WILL do?

_____

_____

ACTIVITY 17

YOUR FATHER

1. What's the best thing about being a parent?

_____

_____

2. What's the worst thing about being a parent?

_____

_____

3. What specific things do you like most about me?

_____

_____

4. What specific things do you like least about me?

_____

_____

5. What about me makes you worry the most?

_____

_____

6. What plans or dreams do you have for me?

_____

_____

7. What makes you glad that I'm growing up?

_____

_____

8. What makes you sad that I'm growing up?

_____

_____

9. Why do you seem to say "NO" so often?

_____

_____

10. Why do you seem to want to know everything about my life?

_____

_____

OR: Why don't you seem to care?

_____

_____

11. What did you do when you were young that you hope I WON'T do?

_____

_____

12. What did you do when you were young that you hope I WILL do?

_____

_____

Predictions

How predictable are your parents? On a scale of 1–10, would you rate them "totally predictable," "totally unpredictable," or somewhere in between? Are they predictable about some things and not others? Do they ever surprise you by behaving very unpredictably?

Read each statement on the following pages. Think about how your parents would react in each of the situations described. Write your predictions — *without* talking to your parents first.

ACTIVITY 18

YOUR MOTHER

1. You completely change your image (your clothes, your attitude, your hair style, the way you talk, and so on).

_____

_____

_____

2. Your best friend is killed in a car accident.

_____

_____

_____

3. You are caught shoplifting. The police bring you home.

_____

_____

_____

4. You win your school's Student of the Year Award.

_____

_____

_____

5. You spend an outrageous amount of money on something you don't really need.

_____

_____

_____

6. You fall in love with someone of a different race.

_____

_____

_____

7. You tell your family that you are about to become a parent.

_____

_____

_____

8. You are suspended from school.

_____

_____

_____

9. You come home early after being out with your friends.

_____

_____

_____

10. Your parents catch you _____ (fill in the blank).

_____

_____

_____

ACTIVITY 18

YOUR FATHER

1. You completely change your image (your clothes, your attitude, your hair style, the way you talk, and so on).

_____

_____

_____

4. Your best friend is killed in a car accident.

_____

_____

_____

3. You are caught shoplifting. The police bring you home.

_____

_____

_____

4. You win your school's Student of the Year Award.

_____

_____

_____

5. You spend an outrageous amount of money on something you don't really need.

_____

_____

_____

6. You fall in love with someone of a different race.

_____

_____

_____

7. You tell your family that you are about to become a parent.

_____

_____

_____

8. You are suspended from school.

_____

_____

_____

9. You come home early after being out with your friends.

_____

_____

_____

10. Your parents catch you _____ (fill in the blank).

_____

_____

_____

LEARNING ABOUT YOUR PARENTS 3

Before doing this activity, be sure to finish Activity #18: Predictions on pages 87–91.

Now interview your parents, asking them the questions on the following pages. (These are the same questions you asked yourself, only here they have been turned into interview questions.) Write down their answers. You may want to invite another family member or a friend to join you for the interviews.

After your interviews, compare your parents' answers with your answers. How accurate were your answers? Did your parents' answers surprise you? How well can you predict their reactions, feelings, and behaviors?

ACTIVITY 19

YOUR
MOTHER

How would you react in each of these situations?

1. I completely change my image (my clothes, my attitude, my hair style, the way I talk, or some other change).

_____

_____

_____

2. My best friend is killed in a car accident.

_____

_____

_____

3. I am caught shoplifting. The police bring me home.

_____

_____

_____

4. I win my school's Student of the Year Award.

_____

_____

_____

5. I spend an outrageous amount of money on something I don't really need.

_____

_____

_____

6. I fall in love with someone of a different race.

_____

_____

_____

7. I tell you that I am about to become a parent.

_____

_____

_____

8. I am suspended from school.

_____

_____

_____

9. I come home early after being out with my friends.

_____

_____

_____

10. You catch me _____ (fill in the blank).

_____

_____

_____

ACTIVITY 19

YOUR FATHER

How would you react in each of these situations?

1. I completely change my image (my clothes, my attitude, my hair style, the way I talk, or some other change).

_____

_____

_____

2. My best friend is killed in a car accident.

_____

_____

_____

3. I am caught shoplifting. The police bring me home.

_____

_____

_____

4. I win my school's Student of the Year Award.

_____

_____

_____

5. I spend an outrageous amount of money on something I don't really need.

_____

_____

_____

6. I fall in love with someone of a different race.

_____

_____

_____

7. I tell you that I am about to become a parent.

_____

_____

_____

8. I am suspended from school.

_____

_____

_____

9. I come home early after being out with my friends.

_____

_____

_____

10. You catch me _____ (fill in the blank).

_____

_____

_____

A NATIONAL FAMILY QUIZ

Take this National Family Quiz to find out what you know about families and family life in your country. Check your answers at the library.

1. What percentage of families are nuclear families in which both parents have jobs? What is the average yearly income of these families?

_____

2. What percentage of families are "traditional" families, where the father has a job and the mother stays home with the children? What is the average yearly income of these families?

_____

3. What percentage of families are single-parent families? What is the average yearly income of these families?

_____

4. On average, how many children are there per family, for all types of families?

_____

5. Is there enough quality day care to meet the need?

_____

6. About how much does it cost to raise a child from infancy to age eighteen?

_____

ACTIVITY 20

7. On average, how old are people when they get married?

_____

8. What is the divorce rate?

_____

9. How many families own their homes?

_____

10. How many families are homeless?

_____

11. What is your country's most famous family? Why do you think they are famous?

_____

12. Do you think there is such a thing as a "typical" family? Is it your family?

_____

YOUR NOTES
AND THOUGHTS

_____

_____

_____

_____

_____

_____

_____

_____

_____

_____

_____

_____

_____

_____

_____

_____

MORE FREE SPIRIT BOOKS

Making the Most of Today:
Daily Readings for Young People on Self-Awareness, Creativity, and Self-Esteem
by Pamela Espeland and Rosemary Wallner
Guides young people through a year of positive thinking, problem-solving, and practical lifeskills.
$8.95; 392 pp; s/c; 4" x 7";
ISBN 0-915793-33-4 / Ages 11 & up

School Power: *Strategies for Succeeding in School*
by Jeanne Shay Schumm, Ph.D. and Marguerite Radencich, Ph.D.
Covers getting organized, taking notes, studying smarter, writing better, following directions, handling homework, managing long-term assignments, and more.
$11.95; 144 pp; s/c; B&W photos;
8 1/2" x 11"; ISBN 0-915793-42-3 / Ages 11 & up

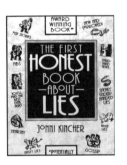

The First Honest Book About Lies
by Jonni Kincher
Discusses the nature of lies and how we live with them every day: at home, at school, in our relationships, and in our culture. Helps kids search for truth, become active, intelligent questioners, and explore their own feelings about lies.
$12.95; 200 pp; s/c; illus.; 8" x 10";
ISBN 0-915793-43-1 / Ages 13 & up

The Survival Guides for Adolescence
by Gail C. Roberts, B.Ed., M.A., and Lorraine Guttormson, M.A.
Help kids confront and cope with their problems, and find answers to their questions. Each book focuses on a different area of concern to young people—family life, school, and stress. The activities call upon kids to be honest with themselves, open to new ideas, and willing to grow. Ages 10–16.

You and Your Family
$8.95; 112 pp; s/c; 8 1/2" x 11";
ISBN 0-915793-24-5

You and School
$8.95; 120 pp; s/c; 8 1/2" x 11";
ISBN 0-915793-25-3

You and Stress
$8.95; 128 pp; s/c; 8 1/2" x 11";
ISBN 0-915793-26-1

A Leader's Guide to You and Your Family, You and School, You and Stress
$6.95; 64 pp; s/c; 8 1/2" x 11";
ISBN 0-915793-27-X

Free Spirit Catalog
Over 70 books, games, and posters on creativity, self-esteem, SELF-HELP FOR KIDS®, and more.

Place
Stamp
Here

FREE SPIRIT PUBLISHING
400 FIRST AVENUE NORTH, SUITE 616
MINNEAPOLIS, MN 55401-1724

400 First Avenue North
Suite 616
Minneapolis, MN 55401-1724
612/338-2068
FAX 612/337-5050

ORDER TOLL-FREE
1-800-735-7323
Monday thru Friday
8:00 A.M.–5:00 P.M. CST

1 ☐ **PLEASE SEND ME THE FREE SPIRIT CATALOG**

2 NAME AND ADDRESS

NAME _____

ADDRESS _____

CITY/STATE _____ ZIP ☐☐☐☐☐

3 SHIP TO (if different from billing address)

NAME _____

ADDRESS _____

CITY/STATE _____ ZIP ☐☐☐☐☐

4 DAYTIME TELEPHONE _____ (in case we have any questions)

5

TITLE	PRICE	QTY.	TOTAL

6 TOTAL

SHIPPING & HANDLING

For merchandise
totals of:.........................Add:
Up to $10.00 ....$3.00
$10.01–$19.99..........$4.00
$20.00–$39.99..........$4.75
$40.00–$59.99..........$6.00
$60.00–$79.99..........$7.50
$80.00–$99.99..........$9.00
$100.00–$149.99....$10.00
$150 or more...............exact
shipping charges

Orders outside continental
North America **add**
$15.00 AIR MAIL

TO RECEIVE A FREE COPY OF THE FREE SPIRIT
CATALOG, OR TO OBTAIN FREE SPIRIT
PUBLICATIONS, PLEASE COMPLETE THIS FORM,
ORDER BY TELEPHONE (1-800-735-7323)
OR ASK FOR FREE SPIRIT BOOKS AT YOUR
LOCAL BOOKSTORE.

7 SUBTOTAL _____

8 SALES TAX (6.5% MN ONLY) **+** _____

9 SHIPPING & HANDLING + _____

10 TOTAL $ _____

METHOD OF PAYMENT

☐ CHECK ☐ P.O. ATTACHED ☐ VISA ☐ MASTERCARD GOOD THROUGH ☐☐ — ☐☐

ACCOUNT # ☐☐☐☐☐☐☐☐☐☐☐☐☐☐☐☐

SIGNATURE _____

THANK YOU FOR YOUR ORDER!

SEND TO: Free Spirit Publishing Inc., 400 First Ave.
North, Suite 616, Minneapolis MN 55401-1724

OR CALL: 1-800-735-7323
LOCAL: 612-338-2068, **FAX:** 612-337-5050

We offer discounts for quantity purchases.
Write or call for more information.